Theory of Music Grade 8
November 2019

AF396010

Your full name (as on appointment form). Please use BLOCK CAPITALS.

Your signature

Candidate number

Centre

Instructions to Candidates

1. The time allowed for answering this paper is **three (3) hours**.
2. Fill in your name and the candidate number printed on your appointment form in the appropriate spaces on this paper, and on any other sheets that you use.
3. **Do not open this paper until you are told to do so.**
4. This paper contains **five (5) sections** and you should answer all of them.
5. Read each question carefully before answering it. Your answers must be written legibly in pen or pencil in the spaces provided.
6. You are reminded that you are bound by the regulations for written exams displayed at the exam centre and listed on page 4 of the current edition of the written exams syllabus. In particular, you are reminded that you are not allowed to bring books, music or papers into the exam room. Bags must be left at the back of the room under the supervision of the invigilator.
7. If you leave the exam room you will not be allowed to return.

Examiner's use only:

1 (30)	
2 (15)	
3 (15)	
4 (20)	
5 (20)	
Total	

(C-08)

Section 1 (30 marks)

1.1   Label this scale: ____

1.2   Write a one-octave Aeolian mode scale starting on B♭, ascending then descending, in a rhythm to fit the given time signature. Use some syncopation between some degrees of the scale. Do not use a key signature but add any necessary accidentals.

1.3   Resolve this French 6th chord for SATB on to the dominant chord and then to the tonic chord of the key signature shown:

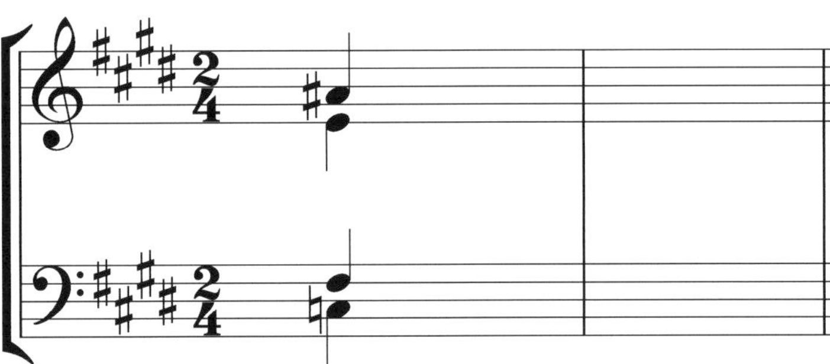

(E major)

1.4   What is the Roman numeral which indicates a dominant 7th chord in its third inversion?

____

1.5   What is an **étude**? ____

____

1.6   Write in groups of four quavers an ascending broken chord of G⁺ᐩ⁷ in the key of E minor.
       Do not use a key signature, but add the necessary accidentals.

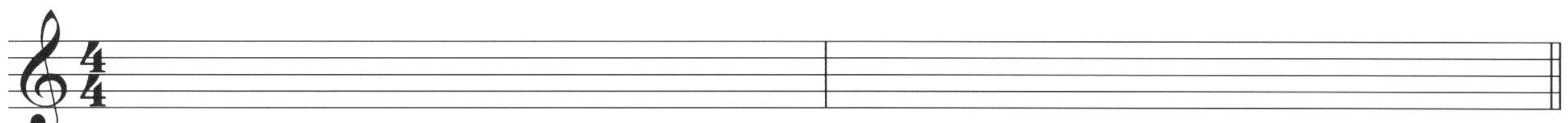

1.7   On the stave below, re-write this tone row in retrograde form:

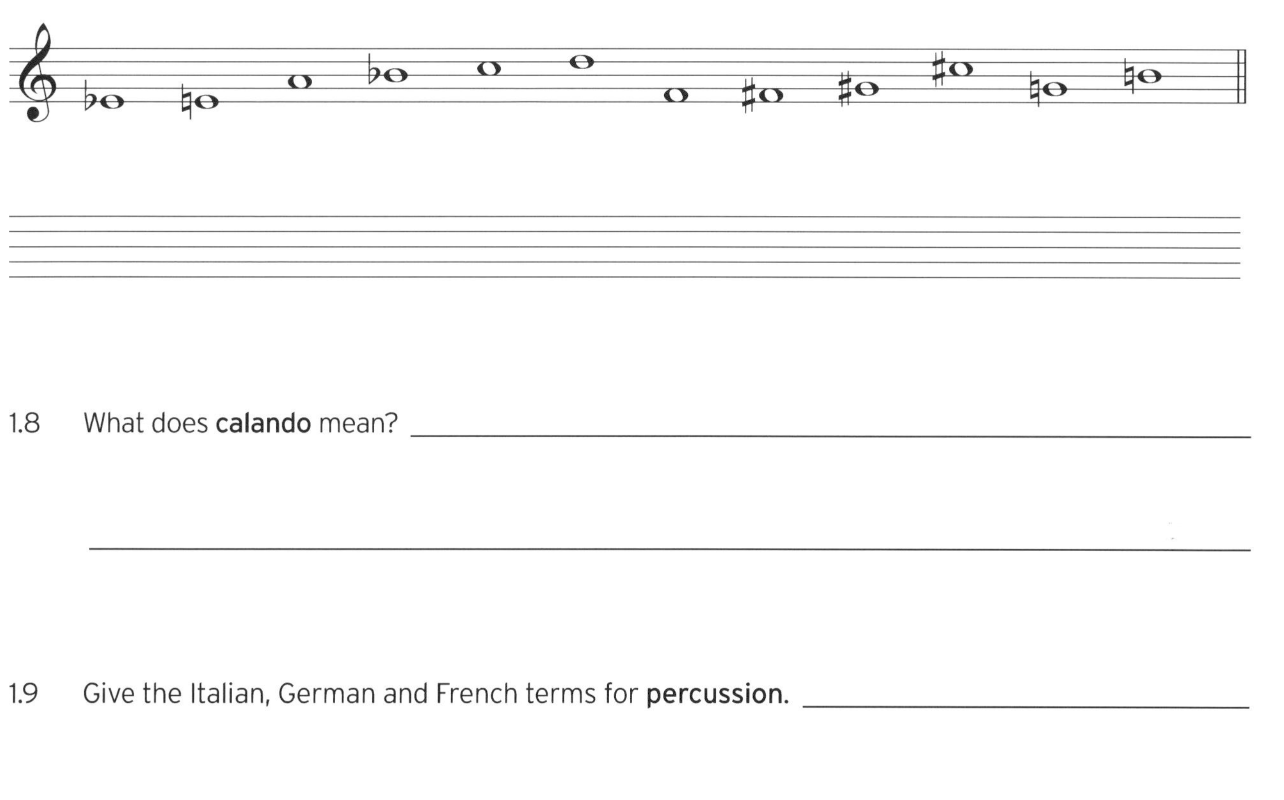

1.8   What does **calando** mean? ____

       ____

1.9   Give the Italian, German and French terms for **percussion.** _____________________

       ____

1.10   Write the notes of a chord (*) which could function as a pivot between this pair of keys:

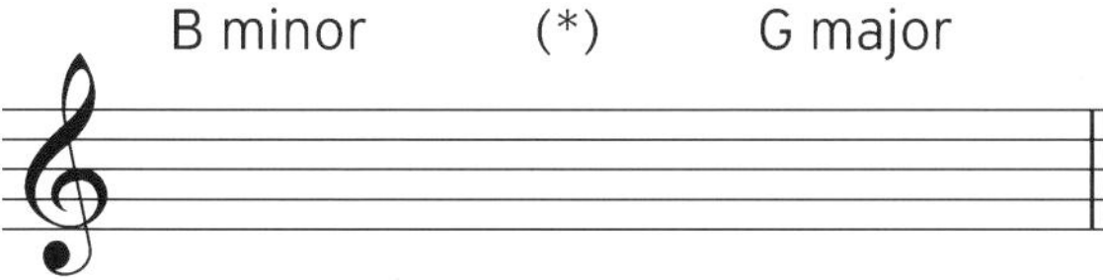

Section 2 (15 marks)

2.1   Write a 12-bar melody in A major for flute. You may use the following as a start if you wish:

Section 3 (15 marks)

3.1   Re-write this passage at sounding pitch (as a score in C) on the staves opposite.

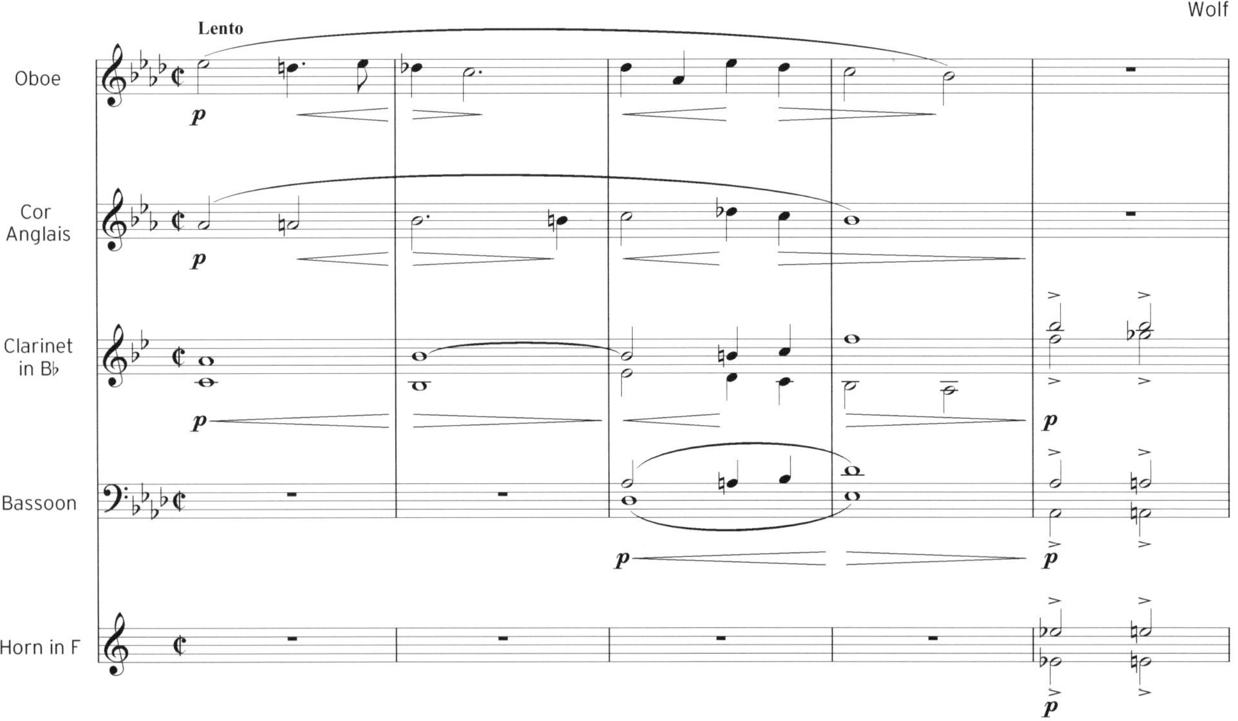

Section 4 (20 marks)

4.1   Harmonise this passage for SATB in an appropriate style, modulating as necessary.

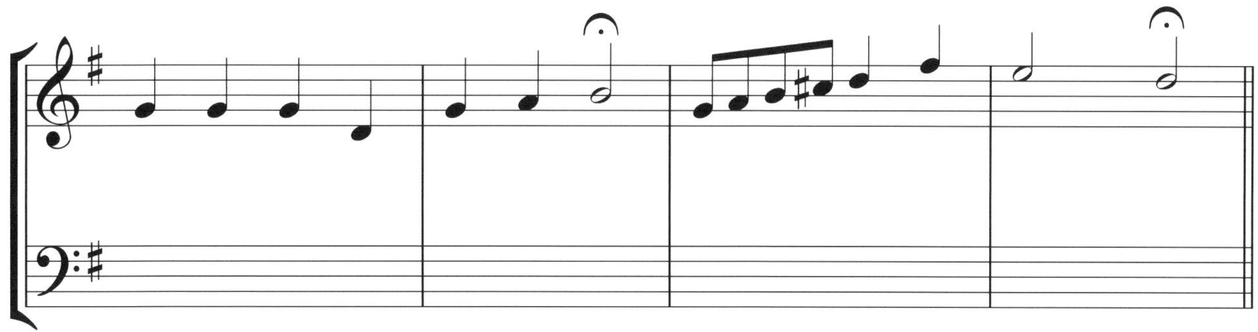

(Please turn over for section 5)

Section 5 (20 marks)

Study this passage and answer the questions opposite.

5.1   Name the key at bar 9. ____

5.2   Put a bracket (⌐¬) over an example of a hemiola.

5.3   Circle a diminished 7th chord.

5.4   How should the chord on the first beat of bar 5 be played? _____________________

____

5.5   Write an appropriate chord symbol above the first beat of bar 18.

5.6   Circle a chromatic auxiliary note in bar 1.

5.7   Write the correct figured bass indication under the last chord of bar 11.

5.8   What does **poco rubato** mean? _______________________________________

5.9   Name the interval between the bracketed (⌐) notes in bar 9._________________________

5.10   Describe the bass part from bar 27 to bar 30. _______________________________

____

Theory of Music Grade 8
November 2019

Your full name (as on appointment form). Please use BLOCK CAPITALS.

Your signature

Candidate number

Centre

Instructions to Candidates

1. The time allowed for answering this paper is **three (3) hours.**
2. Fill in your name and the candidate number printed on your appointment form in the appropriate spaces on this paper, and on any other sheets that you use.
3. **Do not open this paper until you are told to do so.**
4. This paper contains **five (5) sections** and you should answer all of them.
5. Read each question carefully before answering it. Your answers must be written legibly in pen or pencil in the spaces provided.
6. You are reminded that you are bound by the regulations for written exams displayed at the exam centre and listed on page 4 of the current edition of the written exams syllabus. In particular, you are reminded that you are not allowed to bring books, music or papers into the exam room. Bags must be left at the back of the room under the supervision of the invigilator.
7. If you leave the exam room you will not be allowed to return.

Examiner's use only:

1 (30)	
2 (15)	
3 (15)	
4 (20)	
5 (20)	
Total	

(D-08)

Section 1 (30 marks)

1.1 Write in semibreves on the stave below an octave ascending of the Mixolydian mode on E flat. Do not use a key signature, but add the necessary accidentals.

1.2 Name this scale:

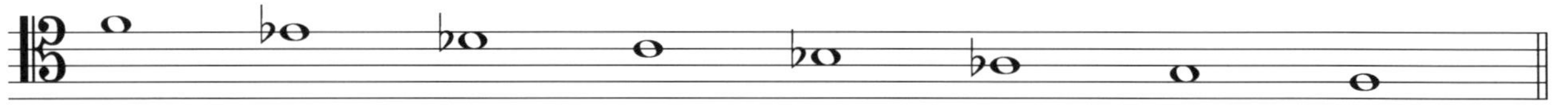

____

1.3 Writing in four parts (SATB), complete the following in the key of B minor to form a passing six-three progression.

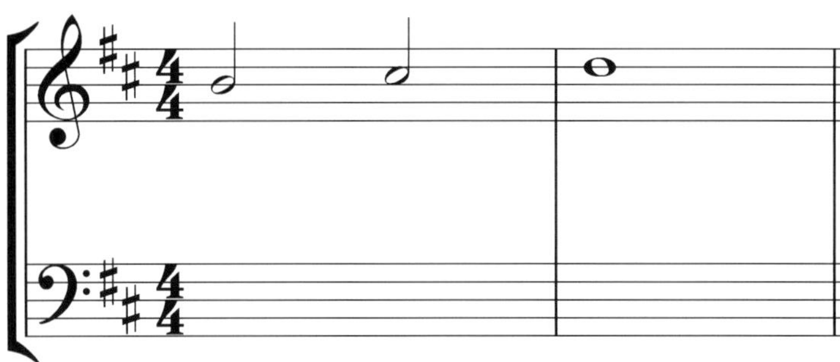

1.4 In which major key do the notes E♭ - G - A - C♯ in ascending order form a French Sixth chord?

____

1.5 Give the correct chord symbol for the chord of ii⁷b in the key of A major.

____

1.6　　What does the interval of an augmented 2nd become when inverted?

1.7　　Name the key of this short passage:

Mozart

1.8　　Write in four groups of four quavers a broken chord ascending of the dominant 7th, first inversion,
　　　　in the key of B major. Do not use a key signature but write in the necessary accidentals.

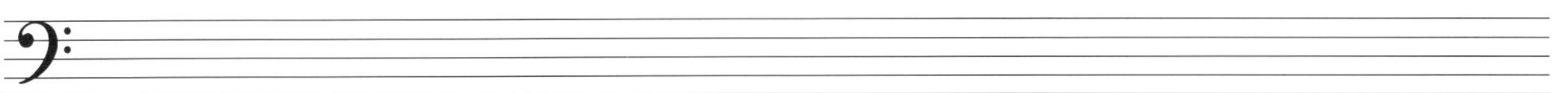

1.9　　What is a **song cycle**?

1.10　　Give the English, French and German names for **ottavino**.

(Please turn over for section 2)

Section 2 (15 marks)

2.1   Write a 12-bar melody in F major for flute. You may use the following as a start if you wish:

Section 3 (15 marks)

3.1   Re-write this passage at sounding pitch (as a score in C) on the staves below.

Section 4 (20 marks)

4.1   Harmonise this passage for SATB in an appropriate style, modulating as necessary.

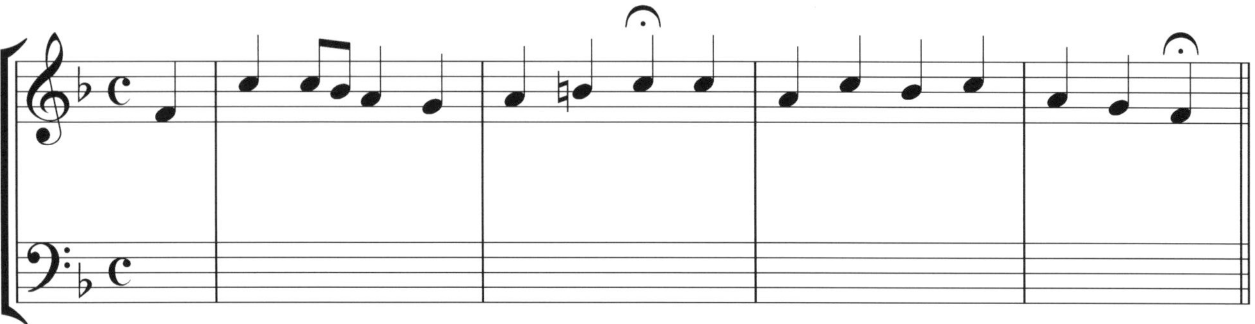

Section 5 (20 marks)

Study this passage and answer the questions opposite.

Haydn

Boxes for
examiner's
use only

5.1   What is the tonic key? ____

5.2   In what key is the cadence in bars 7 (third beat) to 8? _______________________________

5.3   Place the correct Roman numeral beneath the chord on the first beat of bar 5.

5.4   Name the chromatic chord in bar 15 (first beat). _____________________________________

5.5   Write the correct chord symbol above the chord on the first beat of bar 6.

____

5.6   Name the interval between the first two notes (bracketed) in the viola part in bar 15.

____

5.7   Write the correct figured bass indication under the first chord of bar 12.

5.8   Name the cadence in bars 15 (third beat) to 16. ______________________________________

5.9   What kind of note (eg passing note) is the F in the second violin part in bar 3?

____

5.10   What is the overall form of this piece? ____

____

____

THEORY OF MUSIC PAST PAPERS – NOVEMBER 2019 GRADE 8

for Trinity College London written exams

This booklet contains two past exam papers for Trinity College London's Grade 8 exam in music theory, taken from the November 2019 exam sessions. There is no difference in difficulty between the C and D papers.

This booklet can be used in conjunction with the corresponding model answers, which are available to download from **trinitycollege.com/pastpapers**, where you will also find past papers and model answers from other exam sessions.

Download model answers and additional past papers from **trinitycollege.com/pastpapers**

The Theory of Music Workbook series contains all the requirements of the graded exams and provides step-by-step instructions, suitable for use in lessons or for private study. The AMusTCL Study Guide is a practical guide to Section A: Musical skills of Trinity's AMusTCL written diploma. It is also a useful reference guide for anyone wishing to develop their musical knowledge.

Theory of Music Workbook Grade 8	TG 007490	ISBN 978-0-85736-007-6
AMusTCL Study Guide revised 2019 edition	TCL 015853	ISBN 978-0-85736-540-8

Also available from **trinitycollege.com/shop** or your local music shop:

Handbook of Musical Knowledge	TCL 001191	ISBN 978-0-85736-015-1

All syllabuses and further information about Trinity College London exams can be obtained from **trinitycollege.com**

TCL 019905
ISBN 978-0-85736-892-8